J 745.54 Hen
Henry, Sally
Making mosaics

3 4028 07924 9208
HARRIS COUNTY PUBLIC LIBRARY

WITHDRAW
ocn644149302
12/06/2011

$11.75

Making Mosaics

Sally Henry and Trevor Cook

D0913786

PowerKiDS press™

New York

Published in 2011 by The Rosen Publishing Group, Inc.
29 East 21st Street, New York, NY 10010

Copyright © 2011 Arcturus Publishing Limited

All rights reserved. No part of this book may be reproduced in any form without permission in writing from the publisher, except by a reviewer.

Text and design: Sally Henry and Trevor Cook
Editor: Joe Harris
U.S. editor: Kara Murray
Photography: Sally Henry and Trevor Cook

Library of Congress Cataloging-in-Publication Data

Henry, Sally.
 Making mosaics / by Sally Henry and Trevor Cook.
    p. cm. — (Make your own art)
 Includes index.
 ISBN 978-1-4488-1585-2 (library binding) — ISBN 978-1-4488-1617-0 (pbk.) —
ISBN 978-1-4488-1618-7 (6-pack)
 1. Paper work—Juvenile literature. 2. Mosaics—Juvenile literature. I. Cook, Trevor, 1948- II. Title.
 TT870.H426 2011
 745.54—dc22
                                        2010024765

Printed in the United States

SL001622US

CPSIA Compliance Information: Batch #WA11PK: For Further Information contact Rosen Publishing, New York, New York at 1-800-237-9932

Contents

Introduction

Mosaics are artworks in which small pieces of colored stone, glass, or other materials are used to make patterns or pictures. Mosaics have been around since ancient times, and because they are very hard, many historic examples are still around today.

This mosaic portrait of Empress Theodora was made 1,500 years ago in Italy.

Making tiles

Cutting small shapes for mosaic tiles out of glass or stone is very hard and can be dangerous, so we are going to work with materials that are easier and safer to use. The use of color and pattern still works in the same way as with other methods.

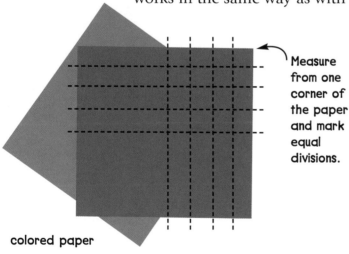

Measure from one corner of the paper and mark equal divisions.

colored paper

A simple way to make tiles (properly called tesserae) is from **colored paper or cardboard**. Draw a grid in pencil on the cardboard. The size of the squares needed varies but is not usually less than .4 by .4 inch (10 x 10 mm). Work from one corner and mark off the divisions using a ruler. Correct measurements at this stage will help you get a good result. Cut the paper or cardboard into strips with scissors, then into individual tiles.

Sometimes you may need to make a special size or shape of tile. They won't always be square. The shape will depend on what you're using them for.

Soft materials

Felt and **fun foam** can be bought from craft stores. Both materials come in bright colors and can be used where soft materials are needed, such as for the planters on pages 16–17 or the jewelry box on pages 28–29.

felt and fun foam

Paint and varnish

To paint your tiles, you'll need a water-based **paint** such as acrylic or tempera. Paint on thick paper or cardboard. Thin paper can wrinkle with water-based paints. When you make **special colors** for projects such as the mosaic portrait on pages 22–23, be sure to make enough for the job. It's better to have too many tiles than to have to match colors later on.

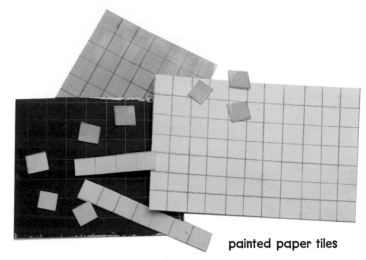

painted paper tiles

Colors show up best when painted over light-colored materials. Strong colors often come out brighter when applied thinly.

water-based paints

When the paint is dry, make the color even brighter with a coat of **varnish**. You can use ordinary water-based household varnishes, either glossy or matte finish. If you are going to fill the gaps in your mosaic, varnish your paper or cardboard first to make it more resistant to the water in the filler and to preserve the colors.

5

Filling the gaps

We use a plaster filler to fill the gaps in the plate mosaic on pages 14–15. You'll need an adult to help with this. You should be able to find a ready-mixed kind that comes in a tube. Read and follow the safety instructions that come with the product. Use a piece of stiff cardboard, plastic, or wood to spread small quantities of filler across your mosaic (we used a popsicle stick). Work it into the gaps and allow it to set. Before it dries, wipe off any excess filler and clean the surface with a wet sponge or cloth. Finally, polish it with a dry cloth.

plaster filler

A good backing

You might spend a long time making your mosaic, so it's important that you build it on something strong and stable. Thick **cardboard** is good for the flat pieces. Corrugated cardboard is bulkier but comparatively light and just the thing for the mats on pages 8–9. Pieces of thin plywood or hardboard are better still for projects such as the portrait on pages 22–23. Get an adult to help you cut things to size.

card stock

cardboard

Natural materials

shells and pebbles

It's possible to make mosaics from natural materials. Look at the pebble pattern on pages 12–13 and the shell mirror on pages 24–25.

Pebbles and **shells** from the seashore don't have the regular shape of mosaic tiles, so they have to be placed very carefully to get an interesting effect. **Sand** is useful as a filling material. Make sure your pebbles, shells, and sand are clean before you use them. Work outside, if possible, and wash everything in clean water, drain them, and leave them to dry. Don't do this in your best clothes, though. It can get messy!

Copying and tracing

If you have to copy a drawing or picture, here's a method that may help. Put some transparent paper (tracing paper) over the photograph or drawing you want to copy. Draw around the important shapes with a soft pencil. Then transfer the drawing onto the new material by turning the tracing over, placing it facedown on the surface, and drawing firmly over the lines again. The pencil line should rub off onto the new surface.

tracing paper

Glue

We've used a glue called **white glue** for most of our mosaic projects. It's white but turns clear when it's dry. Waterproof kinds of white glue are available.

white glue

Use these for projects such as the pebble pattern (pages 12–13), but don't leave them in wet conditions all the time.

rubber cement

To stick paper to paper or paper to card stock, we sometimes use a **glue stick**. It's quick and clean but not as permanent as white glue.

Rubber cement is the best method for sticking flexible things together. We use it to put the badge on the backpack on page 20. Take care not to get it in the wrong place. It won't come off!

glue stick

Tools

A good pair of **scissors** is neccessary for all our mosaic projects. Choose some with safe, rounded tips.

safety scissors

7

A **ruler** with clear markings and straight edges is a useful tool.

We use a **paper punch** to make little round tiles on pages 26–27.

paper punch

Get an adult to help when cutting with a **craft knife**. We use one to cut out frames on pages 18–19.

craft knife

ruler

Clean and safe

Find **somewhere to work** that's easy to clean. Glue is hard to clean off fur and fabrics, so avoid carpets, curtains, and pets. A kitchen is an ideal place, but be sure to ask first. Sometimes there's other work being done there! Put sheets of newspaper down to protect work surfaces. Before you start, it's a good idea to prepare somewhere to put things while they dry.

Animal Mats

Take a simple animal drawing and turn it into a fun and useful mosaic place mat.

60 MINUTES

10 MINUTES

You will need:

- *Tiles cut from colored paper or card stock*
- *Cardboard*
- *Black waterproof marker*
- *Pencil • Scissors • Ruler*
- *White glue • Varnish • Brushes*

What to do...

Draw an outline of an animal from your imagination, or copy our cat or snail. If you're going to cut around your creature, make sure it has its limbs, tail, and head tucked in.

1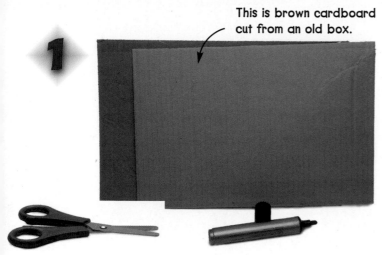

This is brown cardboard cut from an old box.

Cut a piece of cardboard about 8.5 by 11.75 inches (210 x 300 mm). Paint and cut out some tiles, too.

2

Draw your animal on paper first and simplify the drawing as much as you can.

Draw an animal shape on paper or copy one of ours.

3

Draw with a thick black line.

Transfer your drawing to the cardboard and cut around the outside line with scissors.

4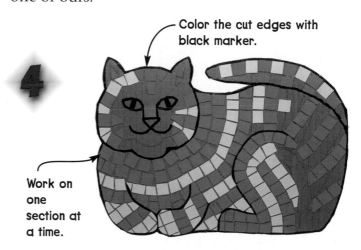

Color the cut edges with black marker.

Work on one section at a time.

Mark simple patterns on the body in pencil. Our cat has a striped tail. Stick the tiles on with white glue. Place the tiles so they touch the black lines without covering them.

5

Varnish makes your mat easy to wipe clean.

Add all the tiles until the animal is complete. Varnish the mat. Do one side first and when it's dry, turn it over and varnish the other side. For extra protection against spills and warm plates, you can get your mats sealed into plastic. Ask about this at your craft store.

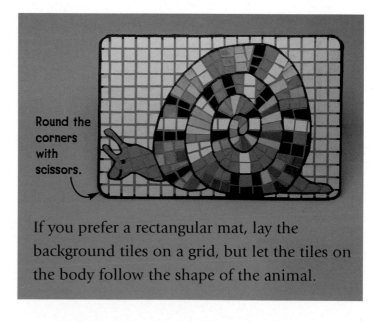

Round the corners with scissors.

If you prefer a rectangular mat, lay the background tiles on a grid, but let the tiles on the body follow the shape of the animal.

Pixel Art

20 MINUTES

10 MINUTES

Computer images are made up of little squares, just like mosaics. Why not make a mosaic of a video game character and hang it on your bedroom door?

You will need:

- *Tiles cut from colored paper*
- *Black cardboard • Glue brush*
- *Scissors • Soft pencil • Ruler*
- *White glue • Sticky putty*

What to do...

Copy our space bug design, or find your own favorite from your computer, a magazine, or a photograph. Start by drawing a grid on the card.

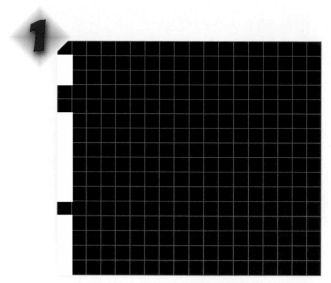

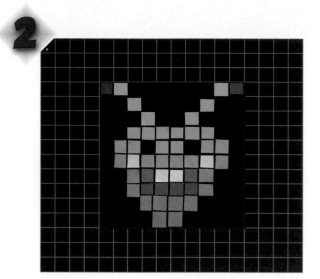

Cut out a piece of black cardboard 18 x 16 units and draw a grid on it with a soft pencil like this.

Cut out some tiles the same size as the squares on your grid. Glue them in the middle.

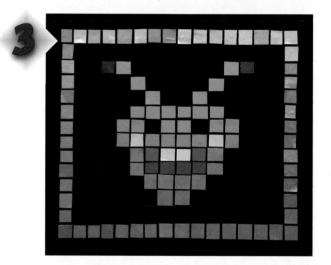

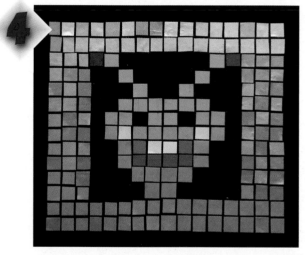

Glue a line of light blue tiles one square in from the edge, to make a frame.

Fill in the rest of the space with more blue tiles. That's the screen done!

To make the keyboard, copy the drawing below onto black cardboard. We've made colored keys, but you can put letters and numbers on yours. How about copying a real keyboard?

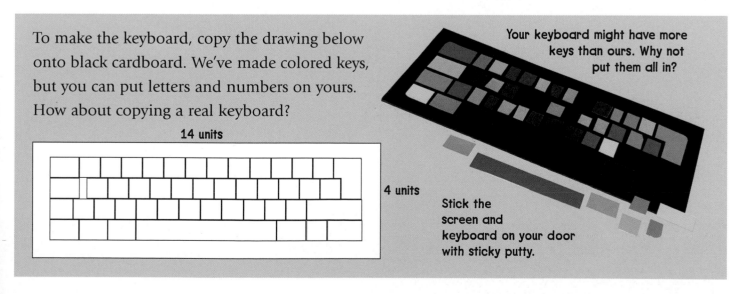

14 units

4 units

Your keyboard might have more keys than ours. Why not put them all in?

Stick the screen and keyboard on your door with sticky putty.

Pebble Pattern

Collect pebbles from the beach to make this garden decoration.

2 HOURS

10 MINUTES

You will need:

- *Plastic tray, the kind that goes under flowerpots*
- *Pebbles, sorted into two or three colors • Sand*
- *Waterproof white glue • Coarse sandpaper*
- *Glue brush • Old paintbrush • Old spoon*
- *Ruler • Black marker • Varnish*

What to do...

Go looking for pebbles that are a similar size and shape. Flat and almond-shaped ones are ideal, but don't worry if you can't find these. The fun is in fitting the shapes together!

1

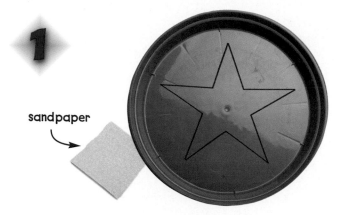

sandpaper

Clean up your pot tray. Roughen the surface of the tray with some sandpaper. Draw a star on the tray with a black marker.

2

Make sure all the pebbles are clean and dry (see page 6). Sort your pebbles into sizes and colors.

3

Start with one color and shape. Glue the pebbles down with waterproof white glue, keeping them packed tightly together.

4

13

Glue a band of dark pebbles around the edge of the tray, then fill in the remaining gap with the third set of pebbles.

5

Thin the white glue with a little water so that it's runny, like milk.

Pour thin white glue through gaps between the pebbles, so that it lies .1 inch (3 mm) deep at the bottom of the tray. Try not to get any on the pebbles, but wipe off any splashes if you do.

6

Clean the sand off the pebbles before the glue dries.

Spoon on dry sand and push it into all the gaps. The glue should soak up through the sand and stick it all together. Allow plenty of time for it to dry, then apply a coat of varnish. It's finished!

Plate Picture

Here's how you can turn a boring old plate into a decoration for your room.

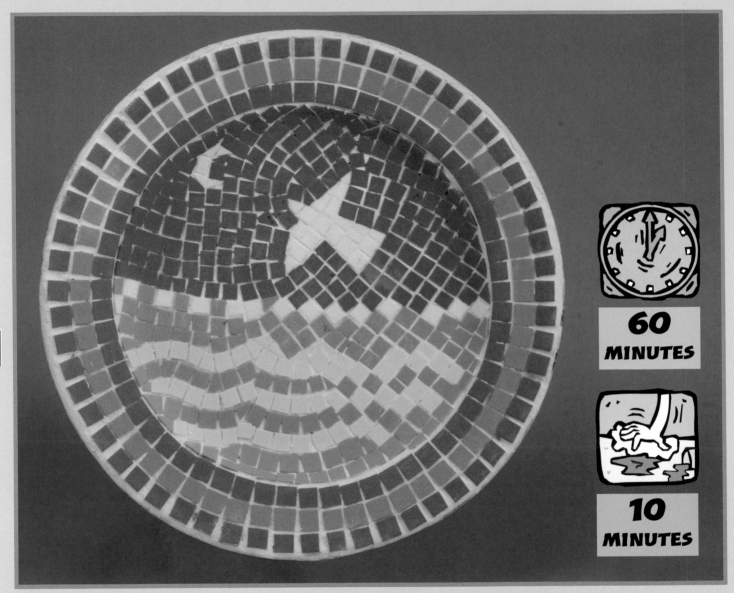

60 MINUTES

10 MINUTES

You will need:

- *Old china or plastic plate*
- *Tiles made of card stock in seven colors*
- *White glue • Brushes*
- *Varnish • Scissors*
- *Plaster filler*

What to do...

It's a good idea to make a mosaic on a plate. The shape goes well with a simple design, and the rim makes a natural frame. Make sure your old plate isn't wanted anymore before you use it. Do ask because changing it into a work of art is permanent!

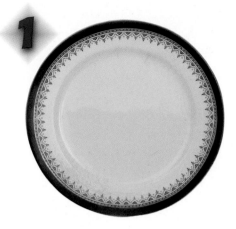

This china plate is a perfect start for a mosaic.

Here's a simple drawing that has just two shapes and five lines!

Cut out tiles, and stick them around the rim with white glue.

Fill in the moon with yellow tiles and the bird shape with white ones.

Fill in the sky with blue tiles. Build out from the edges of the bird.

The lines formed by the gaps between the tiles make an area of flat color more interesting.

Work down from the horizon in light blue and green.

When the whole plate is covered and the glue is dry, coat it with varnish.

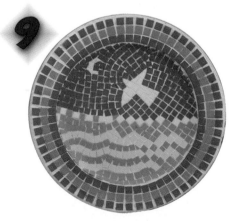

When the varnish is completely dry, fill the gaps with plaster filler (see page 5).

Mosaic Planters

Brighten up those old pots and turn them into something to treasure! An old leaky teapot and a dusty flowerpot both get new jobs as planters. They'll make great gifts for someone!

60 MINUTES

10 MINUTES

You will need:

- *An old container*
- *Tiles cut from six colors of cardboard or fun foam*
- *White glue • Scissors • Varnish*

What to do...

Take a pot, jar, or another container that you are sure nobody wants and scrub it clean. We're going to glue on tiles made of fun foam or cardboard with white glue. The finished pieces aren't weatherproof, but they're just perfect for indoor plants.

1

We're starting with this old teapot. Be careful when working with fragile objects. Always work on a stable work surface. Cut tiles about .5 inch (12 mm) from fun foam or cardboard (see page 4).

2

Build out from the flower.

Start with the important details. We've put a flower on our pot, and it's important that it goes in the middle of one side.

3

When you cover tricky parts like the spout and handle, think about which parts are going to show most and try to get them covered evenly. Under the handle and the spout might be harder to do, but these parts won't be seen so much.

4

Cardboard tiles need a coat of varnish to finish them off. If you used fun foam, don't varnish it. You're finished!

As a quick fix for this dusty old flowerpot, we glued fun foam all over it in a simple, repeating pattern. When you use an old pot like this, it's a good idea to glue a disk of fun foam or felt on the bottom to protect the furniture it stands on.

Wrap tiles over the rim of the pot.

Mosaic Frames

A mosaic frame is the perfect finishing touch to a picture on your bedroom wall.

You will need:

- *Colored card stock*
- *Colored paper*
- *White glue • Cardboard for frames • Scissors • Pencil*
- *Ruler • Paints and brushes*

What to do...

We're going to make borders to use on a flat frame. The patterns came from an idea called a key pattern. You'll need at least two tile colors.

60 MINUTES

5 MINUTES

1

Cut a piece of cardboard 27 units wide and 33 units long. Draw a border 5 units wide. Cut out the rectangle in the middle.

2

Glue colored paper to the cardboard and draw a 27-by-33 grid on it with a soft pencil.

3

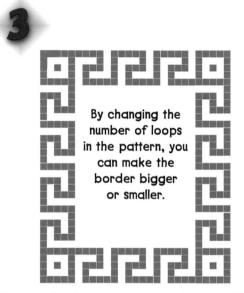

By changing the number of loops in the pattern, you can make the border bigger or smaller.

Gently shade the pattern above with your pencil on the grid.

4

Cut tiles the size of one square unit from card stock or paper (see page 4). Glue the tiles onto the grid. You can start with one color or work with both at the same time as we have here.

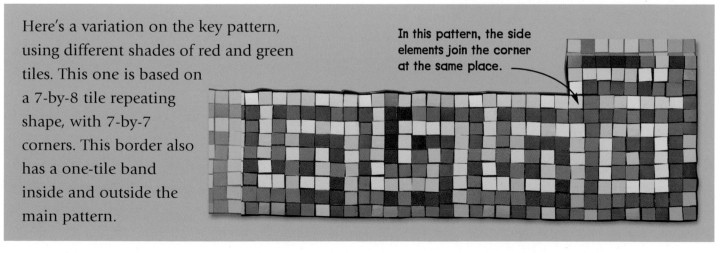

Here's a variation on the key pattern, using different shades of red and green tiles. This one is based on a 7-by-8 tile repeating shape, with 7-by-7 corners. This border also has a one-tile band inside and outside the main pattern.

In this pattern, the side elements join the corner at the same place.

School Bag Mosaic

Surprise your school friends by transforming your backpack! Here's how.

45 MINUTES

5 MINUTES

You will need:

- *Your backpack • Photograph*
- *Fun foam in several colors*
- *Rubber cement • Tape • Pencil*
- *Scissors • Ruler • Tracing paper*

What to do...

Here's how to make a badge to stick on your backpack. Start with a photograph. Make a simple drawing, then cut pieces of fun foam to fit together on the backpack. You can use your own design, or copy ours.

1

Find a photograph that you like and trace over it.

2

Make a simple drawing, divided into shapes.

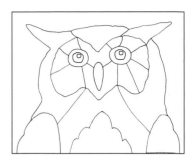

3

Here are the shapes we made from the photograph. You can copy them by tracing (see page 6). The blue lines are the gaps between the shapes, so it's important to cut the shapes very carefully.

4

Cut the green rectangle first, then make the owl-shaped hole in it. As you cut the shapes, check that they fit together properly with the adjoining pieces before sticking them with rubber cement.

Make sure the green shape is straight when you glue it down. You can't change it later!

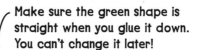

5

It's finished!

Mosaic Portrait

Change a photograph of yourself or a friend into a super mosaic.

75 MINUTES

5 MINUTES

You will need:

- *Gray cardboard* • *White card stock* • *Tracing paper*
- *White glue* • *Paints* • *Varnish* • *Brushes* • *Scissors*
- *Soft pencil* • *Ruler* • *Masking tape* • *Photograph*

What to do...

Find a picture of someone to copy. It can be a friend, a famous person, or just someone you find interesting to look at.

1 Tape the tracing paper to the photograph while you trace.

Choose a photograph that shows the face well.

2

Transfer your tracing to the cardboard background.

3

Paint some card stock with colors taken from the photograph and cut out tiles. Start with the face. You'll need several skin colors.

4

Cut small pieces of tile for details.

Use the lightest-color tiles for highlights on the skin.

Glue on the tiles carefully with white glue. Use it thinly and work quickly.

5

Make sure you have made enough colored tiles for the flat areas of background.

Make more tiles for the rest of the picture. We have covered the background with blue tiles.

6

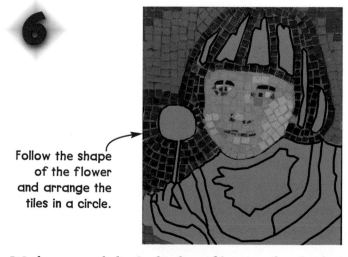

Follow the shape of the flower and arrange the tiles in a circle.

We have used three shades of brown for the hair.

7

When it's finished, brush on clear varnish.

Shell Mirror

Every day will feel like a holiday when you have this mirror on the wall.

90 MINUTES

10 MINUTES

You will need:

- *Small mirror with wide frame*
- *Shells*
- *White glue*
- *Paint and brush*

What to do...

Collect shells if you live near a beach, or buy them at your local craft store. Choose smaller shells, as they will be easier to work with.

1

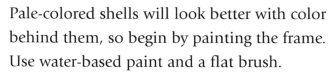
Choose a strong color.

Pale-colored shells will look better with color behind them, so begin by painting the frame. Use water-based paint and a flat brush.

2

We've got large and small shells. Use white glue to stick them down. Glue the larger ones to the middle of each side.

3

Glue the smaller shells in a line all around the edge of the frame. Make sure they all face the same way! Glue a group of three small shells in each corner of the mirror.

4

Fill in the remaining areas with small shells arranged carefully so they flow around the larger shells. When it's all covered, it's finished!

Animal Patterns

The patterns on a turtle's shell and a snake's skin make a great starting point for a mosaic!

2 HOURS

10 MINUTES

You will need:

- Colored paper or card stock
- White glue • Glue brush • Glue stick
- Cardboard for frame • Flat magnet
- Scissors • Ruler • Pencil • Paper punch

What to do...

A snake biting its own tail makes a great frame for a nature picture. If you need a fridge magnet, why not try making the turtle?

1

7.5 inches (190 mm)

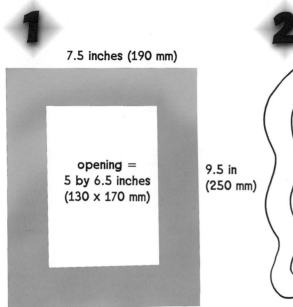

opening =
5 by 6.5 inches
(130 x 170 mm)

9.5 in
(250 mm)

Cut a frame like this in cardboard and cover it with colored paper.

2

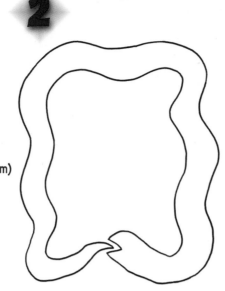

Copy the outline of the snake on card stock the same size as the frame. Our card is black.

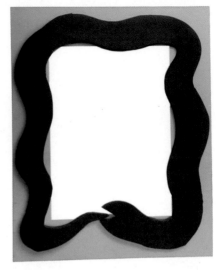

Glue the snake to the frame with white glue.

3

Undo the base to get your tiles out.

Make your mosaic tiles with a paper punch.

4

Don't forget the eye!

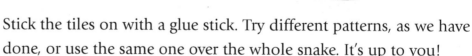

zigzags

stripes

Stick the tiles on with a glue stick. Try different patterns, as we have done, or use the same one over the whole snake. It's up to you!

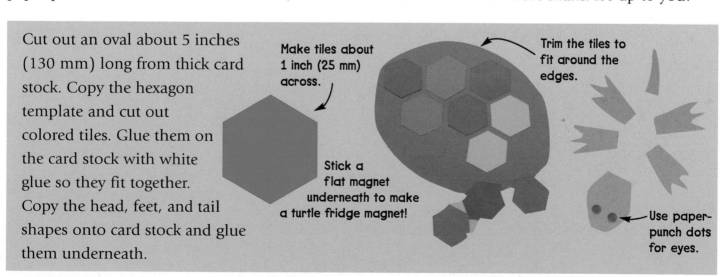

Cut out an oval about 5 inches (130 mm) long from thick card stock. Copy the hexagon template and cut out colored tiles. Glue them on the card stock with white glue so they fit together. Copy the head, feet, and tail shapes onto card stock and glue them underneath.

Make tiles about 1 inch (25 mm) across.

Trim the tiles to fit around the edges.

Stick a flat magnet underneath to make a turtle fridge magnet!

Use paper-punch dots for eyes.

Jewelry Box

This pretty box makes a great gift. What would you keep inside?

You will need:

- *Small cardboard box*
- *Several kinds of fabric*
- *White glue*
- *Paint and brushes*
- *Scissors • Pencil • Ruler*
- *Ballpoint pen*

What to do...

Take a small box that was just an ordinary piece of packaging and turn it into a beautiful gift. We've cut tiles from pieces of rich fabric and arranged them in a mosaic pattern.

30 MINUTES

5 MINUTES

1

Find a box made of cardboard. The outside of the box will show between the tiles when it's finished, so give it a coat of paint.

2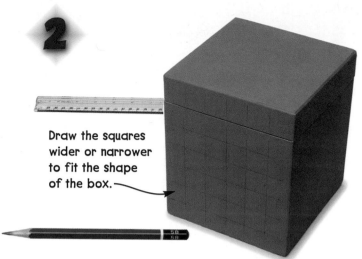

Draw the squares wider or narrower to fit the shape of the box. →

Draw faint grids on the sides and the top of the box with the lines about .75 inches (18 mm). The size will vary with the size of the box.

3

← Draw squares on the back of the fabric with a ballpoint pen.

Cut squares out of several kinds of fabric.

4

Try not to get glue on the surface of the fabric. Keep your fingers clean!

Brush white glue on a small area on the box and carefully press the squares into place.

5

Let one side dry before you start the next.

6

All done! What a great gift for Mother's Day!

Make a Maze or Labyrinth

What's the difference between a maze and a labyrinth? A labyrinth has just one path.

You will need:

- *Cardboard for backing*
- *Colored card stock for tiles*
- *Pencil • Ruler*
- *Scissors*

What to do...

Copy one of the drawings below onto card stock. Fill it in with tiles of two different colors.

60 MINUTES

5 MINUTES

MAZE: 19 x 19 squares

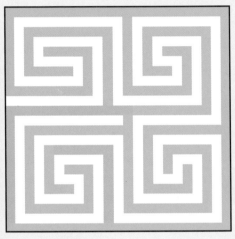

LABYRINTH: 23 x 23 squares

1

Draw a grid on a square piece of cardboard. We're making the second one. It's 23 by 23 squares.

2

You'll need approximately equal numbers of colors for either of the designs. Start gluing on tiles from the top, following the drawing closely. Concentrate hard!

3

When it's finished, you should be able to follow the path from the entrance on the left all the way to the square in the middle, crossing every white square on the way.

Glossary

flexible   (FLEK-sih-bul) Being able to move and bend in many ways.

hexagon   (HEK-sa-gon) A flat shape with six sides.

key pattern   (KEE PA-tern) A kind of pattern found throughout the ancient world based on a repeated simple key shape.

labyrinth   (LA-buh-rinth) A system of passages or paths.

materials   (muh-TEER-ee-ulz) What things are made of.

maze   (MAYZ) A network of paths or passages that is a puzzle to be solved.

portrait   (PAWR-trut) A picture of someone, concentrating on his or her face.

projects   (PRAH-jekts) Special jobs or tasks.

roughen   (RUF-en) To make not smooth.

template   (TEM-plut) An exact version of something that makes it easy to make many copies.

tesserae   (TEH-seh-ree) Little blocks of stone or tile that make up a mosaic.

tracing paper   (TRAYS-ing PAY-per) A special kind of paper that lets you see a picture through it and has a surface that you can draw on in ink or pencil.

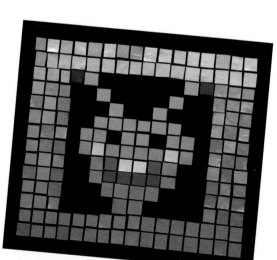

transfer   (TRANZ-fer) To move something from one place to another.

transparent   (tranz-PER-ent) Allowing light to pass through something, so that objects can be seen clearly.

varnish   (VAHR-nish) A special liquid made to put on a surface that then dries and protects it.

Harris County Public Library
Houston, Texas

Index

Web Sites

Due to the changing nature of Internet links, PowerKids Press has developed an online list of Web sites related to the subject of this book. This site is updated regularly. Please use this link to access the list:
www.powerkidslinks.com/myoa/mosaic/